A Bouquet of Love: 100 Valentine's Day Poems

Valentine Philip

Published by Bright Minds Books, 2024.

While every precaution has been taken in the preparation of this book, the publisher assumes no responsibility for errors or omissions, or for damages resulting from the use of the information contained herein.

A BOUQUET OF LOVE: 100 VALENTINE'S DAY POEMS

First edition. December 30, 2024.

ISBN: 979-8230995180

Written by Valentine Philip.

Table of Contents

Description

"**A Bouquet of Love: 100 Valentine's Day Poems**" is a heartfelt celebration of love in its many forms.

Featuring 100 meticulously crafted poems, each with five stanzas of four lines, this collection captures the essence of romance, devotion, and enduring connection. From tender whispers to soaring passions, these verses embrace the timeless beauty of love, offering readers a journey through its highs and depths.

Perfect for Valentine's Day or any moment of reflection, this book is a treasured gift for lovers, dreamers, and romantics alike. Let these poems be your guide to expressing and experiencing love's profound truths.

Dedication

To all who have loved, who love, and who dream of love—
This book is for you.
To those who find joy in a kind word, solace in a gentle touch,
And hope in the promise of tomorrow,
May these poems remind you of love's boundless power
And its ability to light even the darkest paths.
And to my own source of inspiration—thank you for teaching me
That love is the greatest gift we can give and receive.

Preface

Love is universal, yet deeply personal—a force that shapes lives, binds hearts, and fuels dreams. As a poet, I've always been captivated by its myriad expressions: the excitement of new romance, the comfort of lasting connection, and the quiet strength of devotion through challenges. **"A Bouquet of Love: 100 Valentine's Day Poems"** was born from this fascination, a heartfelt attempt to capture love's essence in 100 unique verses.

Each poem in this collection explores a facet of love, from its simplest joys to its deepest complexities. Written with care and a desire to resonate across generations, these poems reflect not only romantic love but also the enduring bonds that connect us all.

Whether shared with a partner, read in solitude, or given as a gift, this book is a celebration of love's transformative power. I hope these words bring as much warmth and inspiration to your heart as they did to mine in creating them.

Poem 1: Whispers in the Rose Garden

In the garden, where the roses bloom,
The air is filled with sweet perfume.
Your laughter dances on the breeze,
A melody that puts my heart at ease.
Your eyes, like stars, they softly gleam,
A vivid light in my every dream.
Each glance a spark, a lover's art,
Igniting warmth within my heart.
Beneath the moon, where shadows play,
We speak of love in soft array.
The night, our witness, calm and still,
As passion bends to our tender will.
Each moment shared, a treasure vast,
A timeless song, a spell is cast.
Together bound, through storm or sun,
Our journey as two souls begun.
In your arms, my worries fade,
A gentle world your love has made.
Forever here, my vow to keep,
With you, my soul finds peaceful sleep.

Poem 2: A Serenade of Hearts

Beneath the willow's gentle sway,
We found our love one golden day.
The leaves whispered secrets, soft and true,
While my heart awoke to the glow of you.
Your voice, a symphony in my ear,
Turns every shadow to something clear.
With every word, you build me high,
A tower of hope against the sky.
Each touch, a canvas, love's sweet hue,
Painted in shades of me and you.
No masterpiece could rival this,
A story told with every kiss.
The seasons turn, but still I find,
Your love is steadfast, sweet and kind.
A refuge strong, my guiding light,
Through every storm, my endless night.
Forever bound, we walk this way,
Through every dusk and dawning day.
A serenade of hearts shall sing,
Of love eternal, a boundless spring.

Poem 3: The Language of Love

You speak in ways the soul can hear,
A tender word, a glance sincere.
No need for sound, your love takes flight,
And fills the void with purest light.
The roses bloom beneath your care,
Each petal soft, beyond compare.
You tend my heart, my garden wide,
With love that grows and will abide.
The stars align within your gaze,
A compass guiding through life's maze.
Your laughter heals, your smile inspires,
A spark that kindles endless fires.
No poet's pen, no singer's tune,
Could capture love beneath the moon.
Yet in your arms, the world makes sense,
A quiet truth, no false pretense.
Each day with you, a line is drawn,
Of love that stretches ever on.
Our story weaves, a tale divine,
Forever yours, forever mine.

Poem 4: The Flame That Never Fades

A single spark began our fire,
A moment born of sweet desire.
Your warmth consumed my lonely cold,
A story of love, timeless and bold.
The winds may blow, the seasons turn,
But still your flame will brightly burn.
Through shadows cast and storms we face,
Your love remains my saving grace.
Each heartbeat speaks a tale untold,
Of passion fierce and courage bold.
Together we have carved a way,
To light the night and grace the day.
The candle flickers, yet it stays,
A constant light in fleeting haze.
No tempest shakes its steady gleam,
A beacon bright, our endless dream.
Forevermore, this vow is made,
To guard the flame that never fades.
Through all of life, my love shall be,
An endless fire for you and me.

Poem 5: A Symphony of Us

Our love is like a melody,
Composed in perfect harmony.
Each note a kiss, each chord a sigh,
A symphony beneath the sky.
The violins of morning play,
When you arise to greet the day.
The soft piano in your voice,
Turns every moment into choice.
The crescendo of your laughter bright,
Illuminates the darkest night.
With every rhythm, sweet and clear,
You bring me joy, you draw me near.
Through life's refrains, its highs and lows,
Our music flows, it gently grows.
Together strong, we'll write the score,
A love that echoes evermore.
And when the final verse is sung,
Our hearts will still be finely strung.
For love like ours will never cease,
A timeless song, a boundless peace.

Poem 6: Roses on the Wind

I sent my love upon the air,
A whisper soft, a secret rare.
Through fields of gold, it found its way,
To rest with you and softly stay.
The petals danced, a scarlet hue,
And carried thoughts I held for you.
Each rose a token, pure and true,
A symbol of my heart's debut.
The breeze that touched your gentle skin,
Was born of passion deep within.
It carried dreams of days to come,
Of love that beats like steady drums.
No distance holds, no time divides,
The bond we share, where love resides.
The wind may blow, the seasons spin,
But roses find you once again.
So hold this truth, my love, my friend,
That roses on the wind won't end.
Forever yours, a vow I give,
In every breeze, my love will live.

Poem 7: The Moon's Secret

Beneath the moon's soft, silver glow,
Our hearts aligned, a tale to show.
Its light caressed your gentle face,
And sealed our love in night's embrace.
The stars above began to hum,
A lullaby where dreams come from.
Each twinkle sang of moments shared,
Of passion pure, of hearts that cared.
The moon, a silent witness still,
Watched over us upon the hill.
Its secret held, its glow serene,
A guardian of what has been.
The tides may rise, the world may change,
But our love stands, it will not range.
A constant force, like lunar pull,
Unchanging, steadfast, calm and full.
So when you see the moon above,
Remember this: it knows our love.
Forever bright, it lights our way,
A beacon for each Valentine's Day.

Poem 8: A Promise in Bloom

I planted seeds within my heart,
To grow a love that won't depart.
With every kiss, the garden grew,
A field of blossoms meant for you.
The violets sang of tender care,
The lilies danced upon the air.
The roses bloomed with hues so bright,
A testament to our delight.
Through summer's sun and winter's frost,
The blooms endured, no love was lost.
Each petal soft, each stem held high,
A promise that will never die.
I'll tend this garden all my days,
With patient hands and love's warm rays.
Through every season, bright or dim,
I'll keep it thriving, full to brim.
So take this bouquet, dearest one,
A gift of love, a life begun.
Each flower whispers soft and true,
My heart forever blooms for you.

Poem 9: Through the Years

Through every trial, through every storm,
Your love has kept my spirit warm.
When shadows fell and doubts took hold,
You gave me courage, strong and bold.
The clock may tick, the years may fly,
But still your love is my clear sky.
With every wrinkle, every line,
I see a love that's truly mine.
We've built a life, a tale of grace,
Each memory leaves a lasting trace.
Through joy and pain, through smiles and tears,
Our bond has deepened through the years.
The seasons shift, the world turns new,
But nothing changes me and you.
Together still, we stand as one,
Our journey's only just begun.
And when our hair has turned to gray,
Our hearts will beat the same each day.
For love like ours is pure and true,
A timeless gift, forever new.

Poem 10: A Love Beyond Words

No words could capture what I feel,
A depth of love, profound and real.
It blooms in silence, speaks in sighs,
A truth reflected in your eyes.
When shadows fall and fears arise,
You are my light, my star-filled skies.
A comfort vast, a steady hand,
You are the ground on which I stand.
Through every moment, joy or pain,
Your love's a calm, a gentle rain.
It heals my wounds, it mends my soul,
And makes my broken spirit whole.
Though poets try, they can't convey,
The boundless love I feel today.
Its language vast, yet soft and true,
Is spoken only between me and you.
Forever more, this vow I make,
To cherish each step we undertake.
For words may fail, but love remains,
A force eternal, unchained by reins.

Poem 11: The Dance of Our Hearts

Beneath the stars, we took our place,
A dance of love, a sweet embrace.
The music soft, the night so still,
Our hearts aligned, our souls fulfilled.
Each step was light, each movement free,
An endless waltz of you and me.
The rhythm spoke what words could not,
A silent vow we'd ne'er forgot.
The world around us fell away,
As love became our sole ballet.
With every spin, with every turn,
The flame within continued to burn.
Though years may pass, our steps remain,
A dance of love through joy and pain.
Together strong, we face the beat,
And find our hearts are ever sweet.
So let the music never cease,
For in your arms, I find my peace.
The dance of hearts, a timeless art,
Forevermore, where love will start.

Poem 12: The Art of Forever

Your love's a canvas, pure and bright,
A masterpiece of morning light.
Each brushstroke soft, a tender hue,
A life we paint, a dream come true.
The palette vast, yet all aligns,
A symphony of vibrant signs.
Your every touch, a perfect shade,
A work of art that love has made.
Through every trial, every tear,
Our masterpiece grows ever clear.
Its beauty lies not in perfection,
But in the truth of our connection.
No artist's hand, no sculptor's stone,
Could craft a bond so deeply known.
For ours is forged by time and trust,
A masterpiece immune to dust.
Together, we will frame our years,
In golden light that love endears.
Our art will stand the test of time,
Forever bound, forever prime.

Poem 13: A Valentine's Dream

I dreamed of you before we met,
A love so pure, with no regret.
The stars had whispered in my sleep,
A promise strong, a bond to keep.
And then you came, a dream made real,
A love profound, a joy to feel.
Your presence turned my nights to day,
And chased my darkest fears away.
No longer dreams, but life so bright,
Each moment shared, a sweet delight.
Our hearts entwined, a perfect thread,
A tapestry of love widespread.
Forevermore, my dream will be,
To hold you close, to keep you free.
A Valentine's wish, each day anew,
To live this dream, my love, with you.
So let us walk where dreams reside,
With hand in hand and hearts as guide.
For every night and morning's gleam,
I'll love you, my Valentine's dream.

Poem 14: A Love Like the Sea

Your love is vast, a boundless sea,
An endless wave surrounding me.
Its depths unknown, its power strong,
A current pulling me along.
The tides may rise, the storms may call,
But still I know you'll catch my fall.
Your love, a calm and steadfast shore,
A place I'll cherish evermore.
The ocean speaks in whispered tones,
Of love that flows through flesh and bones.
Its rhythm steady, pure, and true,
A song composed for me and you.
No tempest shakes this love we share,
Its boundless depth beyond compare.
Together, we will sail as one,
Beneath the moon, beneath the sun.
So let the sea our guide remain,
Through joy, through sorrow, and through pain.
For love like this will always be,
A steadfast, endless, timeless sea.

Poem 15: The Gift of Forever

I sought a gift to give to you,
A token rare, a love so true.
No diamond bright, no golden chain,
Could capture all that words explain.
Instead, I give this vow of mine,
To love you now, through all of time.
Through every storm, through every tear,
My heart will always keep you near.
This gift requires no grand display,
No fleeting charm, no sweet bouquet.
It's wrapped in truth, in hope, in care,
A promise strong, beyond compare.
Each day, this gift will find its place,
In every smile, in every embrace.
It's bound by time, yet freely flows,
A love that deepens as it grows.
So take this gift, my heart, my soul,
The only treasure I can extol.
For all my life, my vow will be,
To give you love eternally.

Poem 16: The Light in Your Eyes

In your eyes, I see the dawn,
A golden glow to build upon.
Each gaze a world, a boundless dream,
A radiant, eternal beam.
They hold the stars, they calm the night,
A beacon strong, a guiding light.
With every glance, my heart takes flight,
Through endless skies, so pure and bright.
No artist's hand, no poet's line,
Could craft a beauty so divine.
Your eyes reflect a love so true,
A mirror of my soul in you.
Through every tear, through every smile,
Your gaze sustains me all the while.
A silent truth, a language rare,
A tender love beyond compare.
Forevermore, my heart shall see,
The light within your eyes, set free.
A fire bright, a soft reprise,
My endless love, your endless skies.

Poem 17: A Valentine's Rose

A single rose, its petals wide,
A symbol of the love inside.
Its crimson hue, a fiery flare,
A love so deep, beyond compare.
Its thorns remind that love takes care,
A careful hand, a heart laid bare.
Yet through the trials, blooms the grace,
A tender bond, a warm embrace.
Each petal whispers soft and sweet,
Of moments where our souls did meet.
The fragrance holds our memories near,
Of laughter shared, of hearts sincere.
A rose may fade, its petals fall,
But love will stand through every call.
Its beauty lies not just in bloom,
But in the light it does presume.
So take this rose, my Valentine,
A gift of love, forever thine.
Its roots are strong, its heart is true,
A flower meant for only you.

Poem 18: Timeless Affection

The clock may tick, the years may fade,
But love endures, unafraid.
Its rhythm steady, pure, and kind,
A melody that binds our mind.
Each moment shared becomes a gem,
A treasure rare, a diadem.
Its luster grows with every year,
A symbol of a bond sincere.
No wrinkle mars, no time erases,
The beauty of love's soft embraces.
Each day a step, a promise made,
In love's warm light, we're unafraid.
Through trials faced, through joy we've known,
Our love has flourished, deeply grown.
A timeless force, a steady flame,
A lasting truth that time won't tame.
Forevermore, I'll stand with you,
Through all the years, our hearts renew.
For love like this will never end,
A timeless gift, my love, my friend.

Poem 19: The Song of Our Love

Our love's a song, a sweet refrain,
That echoes through both joy and pain.
Its melody, both soft and strong,
A tune that lasts our whole life long.
Each verse is built on days we share,
A harmony beyond compare.
Through every trial, every chance,
We find a reason for the dance.
The chorus rises, bold and true,
A celebration of me and you.
Its words are whispered, sung, and told,
A legacy of hearts so bold.
The bridge unites our dreams and fears,
A passage built on love's bright years.
Its notes transform the simple past,
Into a symphony built to last.
So let the music never cease,
A song of love, of joy, of peace.
For in its chords, our hearts reside,
Forever singing side by side.

Poem 20: Love's Gentle Seasons

Our love unfolds like seasons' flow,
A cycle endless, soft and slow.
In spring, it blooms with colors bright,
A tender start, a fresh delight.
Through summer's warmth, it finds its glow,
A fiery sun, a steady show.
Its passion deep, its heart sincere,
A boundless love that draws us near.
In autumn's hue, it learns to rest,
A quiet grace, a life confessed.
Its beauty lies in golden light,
A peace that fills the fading night.
And winter brings its cooling air,
Yet still our love remains a flare.
Through frost and snow, it finds its way,
A steadfast warmth through every day.
Forever turning, yet the same,
Our love endures in every frame.
A gentle cycle, sweet and true,
Each season starts and ends with you.

Poem 21: A Love That Soars

Our love takes flight on eagle's wings,
A boundless force that freedom brings.
It soars above the worldly ties,
To touch the clouds and kiss the skies.
No mountain high, no ocean wide,
Could keep our hearts from being tied.
For in the air, we've found our place,
A boundless love, a warm embrace.
The winds may change, the skies may turn,
But still our hearts will always yearn.
Together strong, we'll face the breeze,
With steady wings and hearts at ease.
Each flight a story, bold and true,
Of all the skies we've journeyed through.
No storm could shake, no gale could break,
The love we share, the vow we make.
Forevermore, we'll soar above,
The earthly bounds with boundless love.
A journey grand, a life explored,
Forever flying, hearts adored.

Poem 22: Love's Eternal Flame

Deep in my heart, a fire burns,
A light that glows, a flame that yearns.
It warms my soul, it guides my way,
Through every night, through every day.
No winds could snuff, no rain could douse,
This steady fire within our house.
It flickers soft, it burns so bright,
A constant in the darkest night.
Each ember speaks of love's pure glow,
Of tender care that we both know.
Its heat unyielding, its spark divine,
A bond eternal, yours and mine.
Through trials fierce, through joy and pain,
The flame of love shall still remain.
Its beauty lies in what it brings,
A warmth that heals, a hope that sings.
Forevermore, this flame will blaze,
A testament to all our days.
No force could dim, no time could tame,
The brilliance of love's eternal flame.

Poem 23: The Thread of Us

A thread unseen, yet tightly bound,
Connects us both in love profound.
Through every turn, through every mile,
It holds us close, it makes us smile.
No scissors sharp, no force could sever,
This thread of love that lasts forever.
Its fibers strong, its colors bold,
A timeless tale we've gently told.
Through tangled paths and winding ways,
It keeps us linked through all our days.
No storm can fray, no strain can break,
This bond we share, this vow we make.
Each knot a memory sweet and true,
A tie that holds me close to you.
It weaves a life, a tapestry,
A love that flows eternally.
So let this thread entwine our hearts,
A bond that never drifts or parts.
Through all of time, it shall endure,
A love unyielding, strong and pure.

Poem 24: A Garden of Love

Our love's a garden, lush and bright,
Where flowers bloom in morning light.
Each petal soft, each leaf aglow,
A world we've nurtured, watched it grow.
The daisies laugh, the violets sing,
Of joy and peace our love does bring.
The roses blush, the lilies sway,
In harmony throughout the day.
Through gentle care, our bond has grown,
A garden lush, a life our own.
No drought can harm, no storm can scar,
The beauty of the blooms we are.
And when the seasons shift and change,
Our love remains, a sweet exchange.
For every root is planted deep,
A promise that we'll always keep.
Forever more, our garden thrives,
A testament to loving lives.
Each flower tells the world our story,
Of endless love and boundless glory.

Poem 25: The Stars We Share

The stars above, so bright and true,
They shine with love for me and you.
Each one a wish, a dream we've made,
A light that will not dim or fade.
We lay beneath the velvet skies,
And see the cosmos in your eyes.
Each twinkle sings of love's embrace,
A perfect glow upon your face.
No distance far, no time too great,
Could break the bond our stars create.
For every night, they softly gleam,
A universe that holds our dream.
Their light will guide us, strong and clear,
Through every trial, every year.
No shadow deep, no night too long,
Could dim the love that keeps us strong.
Forevermore, the stars will say,
Our love is vast, it finds its way.
A galaxy for us to share,
A boundless love beyond compare.

Poem 26: Love's Silent Promise

In quiet moments, hearts do speak,
A language soft, a vow unique.
No words are needed, none are missed,
For love is spoken through a kiss.
Your touch conveys what lips could not,
A silent truth, a tender thought.
Each gesture calm, each moment pure,
A love that's deep and will endure.
No need for songs or grand display,
For love resides in what we say,
Without a word, with just a glance,
A silent promise, true romance.
It's in the way you hold my hand,
A steady force, a soft command.
It's in the warmth your presence brings,
A quiet peace that gently sings.
So let us speak in silent ways,
Through all our nights, through all our days.
For love's true promise softly flows,
In what the heart already knows.

Poem 27: The Beauty of Us

Our love is beauty, pure and rare,
A masterpiece beyond compare.
No sculptor's hand, no painter's brush,
Could craft the bond that makes me blush.
It's in the way you call my name,
A gentle sound that fans the flame.
It's in your laugh, your tender smile,
The moments shared that make life worthwhile.
Each day with you, a work of art,
A portrait painted from the heart.
Its colors rich, its strokes divine,
A canvas drawn by love's design.
No critic's eye, no fleeting trend,
Could judge the beauty love does send.
For in our bond, the truth does rest,
That love's pure beauty is the best.
Together we will paint the years,
With vibrant hues and joyful tears.
A masterpiece of life we'll make,
A beauty no one else could fake.

Poem 28: Love's Gentle Wings

Our love takes flight on gentle wings,
A fragile grace that softly sings.
It soars through skies, serene and blue,
A bond that's vast and ever true.
Each flutter speaks of tender care,
A whisper carried on the air.
With every beat, the winds do rise,
And lift us up to endless skies.
No storm can ground the love we share,
It finds the light, no matter where.
Through clouds and rain, through sunlit streams,
Our love will glide on boundless dreams.
Together strong, we rise above,
Two souls entwined in fearless love.
Through every flight, we find our way,
A journey endless, come what may.
Forevermore, these wings will keep,
Our love aloft, awake, not asleep.
A gentle force, a hopeful song,
Through skies eternal, where we belong.

Poem 29: The Shoreline of Us

Upon the shore where waves collide,
I found my home, my love, my guide.
The ocean spoke in whispers low,
Of tides that ebb and hearts that grow.
The sand beneath, a fleeting grace,
Yet still our love has found its place.
Each footprint left, a mark of time,
A testament to love's design.
The waves may crash, the winds may howl,
But still our love will not disavow.
For every tide that pulls away,
Brings it back stronger the next day.
We walk the shore, hand clasped in hand,
Our hearts aligned, our spirits grand.
Through every sunrise, every swell,
Our story's one the sea will tell.
Forever bound by ocean's song,
The shoreline of us, where we belong.
A place of love, a tranquil hue,
A world of dreams shared by me and you.

Poem 30: Love's Eternal Spring

In every bloom, in every tree,
I find the love you've given me.
A garden vast, a meadow wide,
Where love does blossom, where dreams reside.
The daffodils, with golden hue,
Reflect the warmth I've found in you.
The lilacs scent the air with grace,
A mirror of your sweet embrace.
The springtime sings of love's delight,
Of mornings fresh and starry nights.
Its beauty lies in life anew,
A love that grows in all we do.
No frost could steal this gentle land,
No drought could break what we have planned.
For in your heart, I've found my home,
A garden vast, my sacred poem.
Forevermore, we'll tend this spring,
Through every joy the seasons bring.
A love that blooms, a boundless thing,
An endless, heartfelt offering.

Poem 31: The Warmth of Your Smile

The warmth of your smile, it melts the frost,
A radiant glow that's never lost.
It lights my path when days grow dim,
A guiding star, a hopeful hymn.
Your laughter rings like silver chimes,
A music pure that halts all time.
Each note a gift, each tone sincere,
A melody I long to hear.
No shadow lingers, no fear abides,
When I am held by your bright tides.
Your joy becomes my gentle shield,
A power strong, a love revealed.
Through every storm, your smile remains,
A beacon bright in life's domains.
It warms my soul, it heals my pain,
And brings me peace in every vein.
Forever yours, I'll stand in awe,
Of every grace your smile will draw.
A timeless gift, a light to see,
A love unending, wild and free.

Poem 32: Love's Guiding Star

Beneath the sky, so vast and clear,
I found my love, my compass near.
Through every storm, through endless night,
Your love became my guiding light.
No path too dark, no road too steep,
Your steady glow my heart does keep.
It shines with hope, with care profound,
A beacon strong, where peace is found.
The stars may fall, the heavens fade,
But love like ours will not dissuade.
It holds the course, it stays the way,
Through every turn, through night and day.
Together strong, we'll chart the skies,
A journey vast where true love flies.
No storm can break, no force unbind,
The guiding star we've come to find.
Forevermore, your light shall be,
The star that leads me endlessly.
A love so vast, a flame so bright,
A gift of hope, my heart's delight.

Poem 33: The Depths of Our Love

Our love's a sea, so vast and deep,
A boundless world where dreams do sleep.
Its waters calm, its tides serene,
A beauty rare, a life unseen.
The ocean sings of love profound,
A melody that knows no bounds.
Its waves, they carry all we share,
A love that's true, beyond compare.
The storms may come, the skies may cry,
But still our love will never die.
Its depths untouched, its heart alive,
A force that helps us both survive.
No compass points, no map can show,
The depths to which our hearts will go.
Together strong, we'll always swim,
Through waters vast, through edges dim.
Forevermore, the sea will say,
Our love's a tide that finds its way.
A boundless depth, a truth unspoken,
An endless ocean, never broken.

Poem 34: A Love That Shines

Your love, a light that guides my soul,
A radiant fire, pure and whole.
Through darkest nights, it softly gleams,
A glow that fuels my wildest dreams.
It dances bright, a beacon clear,
Dispelling every doubt and fear.
Its brilliance warms, its strength inspires,
A spark that sets my heart on fire.
No shadow deep, no mist too wide,
Could dim the light you keep inside.
It shines through storms, it cuts the haze,
A constant force through endless days.
Together we, like stars, will burn,
A love that never will return.
Its brilliance vast, its truth untamed,
A force eternal, unrestrained.
Forevermore, your light will be,
A boundless gift, a legacy.
A love that shines, so pure, so strong,
A flame that burns our whole life long.

Poem 35: A Bond Like Gold

Our love, a treasure rich and rare,
A precious bond beyond compare.
Like molten gold, it bends, it molds,
A warmth that every moment holds.
It gleams with care, it shines with grace,
A beauty time cannot erase.
Its value lies not in its gleam,
But in the heart of every dream.
No pressure great, no weight could break,
The strength of what our hearts create.
This bond endures, it shall not fail,
Through every joy, through every gale.
Together strong, we guard this trove,
A vault of memories, built by love.
Its riches vast, its worth untold,
Our love, a bond as pure as gold.
Forever yours, forever mine,
A treasure kept through space and time.
No force could steal, no age could fade,
The masterpiece our hearts have made.

Poem 36: The Strength of Our Love

Our love is strong, it will not break,
Through every trial, for your sake.
It bends, it sways, but never falls,
A force that answers every call.
Through storms and winds, it stands its ground,
A fortress where our hearts are found.
No weight too great, no loss too keen,
Could sever what our bond has seen.
The strength we share is built on care,
On trust that grows with every prayer.
It's rooted deep, it reaches high,
A towering love that scrapes the sky.
No fear can shake, no doubt can sway,
The steadfast love we share each day.
Its power vast, its promise clear,
A shelter strong, forever near.
So let the world do as it may,
Our love will stand, come what may.
Through every trial, hand in glove,
We'll find the strength within our love.

Poem 37: A Heart That Speaks

Your heart, it speaks without a sound,
A language deep, a love profound.
Each beat a word, each thrum a phrase,
A poem of life, a song of praise.
It tells of care, it sings of peace,
A truth that grows and will not cease.
No sweeter voice could I have heard,
Than what your heart says with no word.
In quiet nights, I hear its call,
A steady rhythm, through it all.
It whispers love, it hums of grace,
A melody time won't erase.
Together, let our hearts align,
Their songs become a hymn divine.
No force could stop their sweet duet,
A harmony we won't forget.
Forevermore, your heart shall be,
The voice that speaks my love to me.
A soundless truth, a silent creed,
The only voice I'll ever need.

Poem 38: The Fire in Your Touch

Your touch, a fire, so warm, so bright,
It sets my world alight each night.
A simple brush, a fleeting spark,
Turns shadows bright, ignites the dark.
It tells a tale of love so pure,
A gentle warmth that will endure.
No frost could chill, no ice could tame,
The burning fire within its flame.
Each time we touch, my heart takes flight,
A comet streaking through the night.
Its blazing trail, a mark of you,
A love that's vast, a passion true.
No fire burns as fiercely strong,
As what I've felt in your touch long.
Its heat a haven, soft yet wild,
A force that's tender, sweet, and mild.
Forever yours, this fire will stay,
Through winter's frost, through summer's ray.
Its glow a gift, its warmth so true,
A fire kindled by only you.

Poem 39: A Love That Grows

Our love's a seed, so small, so bright,
It blooms with care, it finds the light.
Through fertile ground and gentle rain,
It stretches forth despite the strain.
Its roots run deep, its stem stands tall,
It weathers every rise and fall.
No drought can break, no storm can sway,
The growth of love we plant each day.
Each leaf unfolds, each petal shines,
A testament to hearts entwined.
Through every season, green or gold,
Our love will thrive, it won't grow old.
The garden vast, the blooms are rare,
Yet each reflects the bond we share.
A miracle of life renewed,
A living hope, a love imbued.
Forevermore, our hearts will sow,
A field of love that will not go.
Through rain and sun, through joy and woes,
We'll nurture what forever grows.

Poem 40: The Melody of Us

Our love's a melody so sweet,
A tune where two hearts softly meet.
Each note a step, each chord a dance,
A symphony of pure romance.
The violins of tender care,
Compose a song beyond compare.
The drums of passion boldly play,
A rhythm strong through night and day.
Through minor keys and crescendos,
Our song persists, it only grows.
Its beauty lies in what we share,
A harmony that's always there.
No silence breaks this endless song,
Its music plays where we belong.
Together strong, we hold the line,
A love eternal, pure, divine.
Forevermore, we'll let it ring,
A timeless, boundless song we sing.
The melody of us will stay,
A tune of love in every way.

Poem 41: A Love Unbroken

No force could break the love we've made,
No shadow dim, no light could fade.
Through trials fierce, through skies turned gray,
Our love endures, it finds its way.
Each crack we've healed, each tear we've sewn,
Has made our bond a truth well-known.
Its strength resides in hearts that trust,
A foundation firm, a bond robust.
Though winds may howl, though seas may rise,
Our love will stand, a force so wise.
Its walls are built with care and pride,
A refuge safe where we abide.
Through every storm, through every quake,
This love of ours will never break.
It holds us close, it lifts us high,
A bond unbroken, reaching sky.
Forevermore, through all that's true,
My heart will always anchor you.
Together strong, we'll face the tide,
Our love unbroken, unified.

Poem 42: The Kiss of Forever

A single kiss, so soft, so sweet,
It lingers long where our lips meet.
A spark ignites, a world takes flight,
A moment pure, a love so right.
Each kiss a vow, a truth we share,
A silent pledge, a gentle care.
No words are needed, none could say,
What love conveys in its own way.
Through every kiss, our hearts align,
A timeless rhythm, yours and mine.
No fleeting thing, no passing thrill,
But a tender force that time won't kill.
It seals our dreams, it binds our days,
It lights the path through life's vast maze.
A kiss, a gift that love does bring,
A mark eternal, an endless ring.
Forevermore, each kiss shall be,
A thread that weaves our destiny.
A bond so true, a tie so strong,
The kiss of forever, our lifelong song.

Poem 43: A Love That Heals

Your love, it heals my deepest scars,
It mends my heart, it reaches far.
Its touch a balm, its care a cure,
A strength so tender, calm and pure.
Through every ache, through every tear,
Your love has held me, brought me near.
No wound too deep, no hurt too wide,
That love cannot restore inside.
It speaks of peace, it breathes of care,
It lifts my soul from dark despair.
A gentle force, it soothes my pain,
And fills my world with light again.
No greater gift could I have known,
Than love that claims me as its own.
It builds me up, it sets me free,
A healing grace eternally.
Forevermore, your love will stay,
A light that heals in every way.
Through life's great trials, through joy revealed,
I'll cherish love that gently heals.

Poem 44: The Gift of Us

Our love, a gift so deeply rare,
A bond that time cannot impair.
It's wrapped in trust, in ribbons wide,
A present meant to never hide.
Each moment shared, a treasure found,
A joy that knows no earthly bound.
Its worth is more than gold could hold,
A story bright, a truth retold.
No fleeting thing, no passing thrill,
But love enduring, strong, and still.
It holds the power to renew,
A gift unwrapped in me and you.
Together we will guard this prize,
A love that blooms, that never dies.
Its beauty lies in what we give,
A shared delight, a life to live.
Forevermore, this gift will be,
A symbol of eternity.
The gift of us, so sweet, so true,
A priceless bond, just me and you.

Poem 45: The Language of Us

We speak a tongue the world can't hear,
A language rare, profound, sincere.
No need for words, no need for sound,
Our hearts converse where love is found.
Each glance, a sentence; each smile, a line,
A silent prose, a bond divine.
The way you hold, the way you stay,
It tells me all you wish to say.
Through every trial, every test,
Our love's unspoken truths attest.
Its grammar rich, its cadence sweet,
A dialect where souls do meet.
No dictionary could define,
The language shared by yours and mine.
Its meaning vast, its beauty grand,
A script we write with hearts in hand.
Forevermore, we'll weave this art,
A speech that binds both soul and heart.
The language of us, a timeless tune,
A love that sings beneath the moon.

Poem 46: A Love Like Rain

Your love, it falls like gentle rain,
A soothing balm to ease my pain.
Each droplet soft, each stream a song,
A melody that plays lifelong.
It quenches thirst, it fills the air,
A steady force that's always there.
No drought could stop its constant flow,
A love that lives, a love that grows.
The storm may rage, the thunder roar,
But still your love will softly pour.
Through every trial, through every fear,
It washes doubt, it draws me near.
Each tear you dry, each ache you heal,
Your rain reveals the love you feel.
Its endless stream, its boundless care,
A gift of life beyond compare.
Forevermore, your rain will stay,
A blessing in both night and day.
A love like rain, so pure, so true,
Forever falling, born of you.

Poem 47: The Strength of Us

Through every storm, through every gale,
Our love has stood, it will not fail.
Its roots are deep, its branches wide,
A fortress strong where hearts reside.
No winds can shake, no waves can sweep,
The strength of what our hearts do keep.
It holds us firm, it lifts us high,
A love that climbs toward the sky.
Through cracks and flaws, we've built anew,
A stronger bond that's tried and true.
No trial fierce, no pain too great,
Could ever shatter what we create.
Together bold, we'll face the tide,
With love's pure strength as our guide.
Through every battle, hand in hand,
A force unbroken, we will stand.
Forevermore, we'll prove this truth,
A love eternal, strong in youth.
The strength of us, a power rare,
A bond unyielding, beyond compare.

Poem 48: The Flame of Forever

Our love's a flame, so warm, so bright,
It flickers gently through the night.
No wind could snuff, no chill could tame,
The fire born of love's sweet name.
It starts with sparks, it grows with care,
A blaze that warms the coldest air.
Its embers glow, its heat remains,
Through every joy, through every pain.
No shadow dark, no winter's frost,
Could ever see this fire lost.
Its brilliance burns, its light extends,
A beacon where our journey bends.
Together we will fan its flame,
Through every trial, through every name.
It fuels our life, it lights our way,
A fire that never fades away.
Forevermore, this flame will shine,
A love eternal, yours and mine.
A warmth that fills each fleeting hour,
A fire built on love's sweet power.

Poem 49: A Love Beyond Time

Our love defies the clock's decree,
A bond that spans eternity.
No ticking hand, no fleeting day,
Could take this timeless love away.
It blossoms fresh with every year,
A force unchanging, always near.
Its roots are deep, its branches high,
A love that stretches to the sky.
No age could dull, no years erase,
The endless glow of your embrace.
Each moment shared, a treasure bright,
A spark of joy, a beam of light.
Together we, beyond the frame,
Will carve a path through love's sweet flame.
No end in sight, no limit known,
This love of ours forever grown.
Forevermore, our hearts entwine,
A love unbound by space or time.
A story vast, a tale so true,
Eternal life in loving you.

Poem 50: The Heart of the Storm

When thunder rolls and lightning strikes,
Your love becomes the calm I like.
Through raging winds and skies of gray,
You are my shelter, my steady bay.
No tempest fierce could pull apart,
The steady beat of your strong heart.
It holds me safe, it lifts me high,
A beacon strong beneath the sky.
Each drop of rain, each howl of gale,
Is met with love that will not fail.
It carries me through waves untamed,
And soothes my soul when I'm inflamed.
The storm may rage, the world may spin,
But love like ours will always win.
A refuge built on trust and care,
A place of peace that's always there.
Forevermore, you'll be my calm,
My steady strength, my healing balm.
Through every storm, your heart will stay,
My guiding light, my night and day.

Poem 51: A Love Like Springtime

Your love's a breeze of sweet perfume,
A burst of life, a springtime bloom.
It brightens skies, it wakes the earth,
It shows me love's unending worth.
The daffodils, with golden hue,
Reflect the light I see in you.
The cherry blossoms, soft and rare,
Mirror the joy we've come to share.
Each day with you, a season bright,
A gentle touch, a pure delight.
Through April rains and skies of blue,
My world renews because of you.
No winter frost could chill this glow,
For love like ours will always grow.
It stretches forth, it finds its way,
Through every dawn, through every day.
Forevermore, this spring will shine,
A season sweet, a love divine.
Through every bloom, through life's new song,
Our springtime love will last lifelong.

Poem 52: The Depth of Your Love

The depth of your love, so vast, so wide,
A boundless sea where dreams reside.
Its waters calm, its waves serene,
A beauty rich, a force unseen.
No chart could measure, no line could trace,
The depth of love within your grace.
It reaches far, it dives so deep,
A treasure vast for me to keep.
Each wave that crests, each tide that flows,
Speaks of the love that always grows.
No storm can churn, no wind can sway,
The steady tide that finds its way.
Through every ocean's ebb and flow,
Your love remains, a truth I know.
Its depth profound, its beauty rare,
A sea of love beyond compare.
Forevermore, I'll swim this sea,
A place of peace, of love, of we.
The depth of your love, my safe abode,
A boundless world where hearts explode.

Poem 53: A Love That Glows

Your love, it glows like morning light,
A radiant warmth, a pure delight.
It fills the air, it wakes the dawn,
It greets each day, a beauty drawn.
Its glow reflects in all you do,
A kindness vast, a heart so true.
No shadow lingers, no darkness stays,
When love like yours lights up my days.
Each smile you give, each word you say,
Turns every night into bright day.
Its glow so soft, its care so strong,
It leads my heart where I belong.
Through every trial, through every tear,
Your love remains, it holds me near.
A light that heals, a fire that burns,
A constant glow my soul returns.
Forevermore, your love will shine,
A beacon bright, forever mine.
A glowing warmth, a steady fire,
A love that lifts, that will inspire.

Poem 54: A Love Like the Sky

Your love's as vast as skies above,
A boundless realm of endless love.
Its hues of blue, its clouds so white,
Reflect a heart both calm and bright.
No storm can dim its vibrant glow,
No distance far could make it go.
It stretches far, it reaches high,
A love eternal, like the sky.
Each sunrise sings of love's embrace,
Each star reveals its boundless grace.
Through every dawn, through every hue,
The sky reminds me, I have you.
No limits bind, no edges hold,
The love we share, so brave, so bold.
Its beauty lies in how it grows,
A sky of dreams where true love flows.
Forevermore, your love will be,
A sky of hope, of unity.
A canvas vast where hearts can fly,
A love as endless as the sky.

Poem 55: The Light of Our Love

Our love, a light that softly glows,
Through every path that life bestows.
It warms the night, it leads the day,
A guiding star to show the way.
No shadow falls where love does shine,
Its brilliance pure, its touch divine.
Through every doubt, through every fear,
Its glow remains, forever near.
A lantern bright, a steadfast flame,
It lights the way, it calls my name.
Its gentle rays, its tender gleam,
Illuminate my every dream.
Together strong, we hold this light,
Through darkest hours, through longest night.
Its power vast, its beauty true,
A love that shines in all we do.
Forevermore, this light will guide,
A love that cannot be denied.
Its glow a force, its warmth a flame,
A beacon strong in love's sweet name.

Poem 56: The Rhythm of Us

Our love's a rhythm, soft and slow,
A steady beat where dreams do grow.
Its cadence sweet, its pace divine,
A melody of you and mine.
Each heartbeat hums, each moment sings,
Of love that soars on timeless wings.
No faster tune, no fleeting pace,
Could match this song of our embrace.
Its tempo builds, its echoes stay,
Through every turn, through night and day.
A symphony that life imparts,
A rhythm written in our hearts.
Through highs and lows, through silence clear,
Our love's sweet rhythm draws me near.
It keeps us close, it holds us true,
A pulse of life for me and you.
Forevermore, this song will play,
A timeless rhythm, come what may.
The music of us, a perfect art,
A love that beats from heart to heart.

Poem 57: The Power of Love

Your love, it holds a mighty power,
A strength that grows with every hour.
It lifts me high, it keeps me near,
A force that conquers every fear.
No mountain steep, no valley low,
Could block the way your love does go.
It breaks the chains, it clears the skies,
A power strong that never dies.
Through every trial, it prevails,
A wind that fills my hopeful sails.
Its might a gift, its grace untold,
A power pure, a strength of gold.
Together strong, we build, we rise,
A force that reaches to the skies.
No doubt could shake, no fear could quell,
The power of love we know so well.
Forevermore, this strength will stay,
A mighty force through night and day.
The power of love, so vast, so true,
Will always live in me and you.

Poem 58: The Beauty of Forever

The beauty of forever lies,
In love that never says goodbyes.
Its endless glow, its steady stream,
A boundless force, a perfect dream.
No fleeting joy, no passing thrill,
But love that grows and lingers still.
Its beauty shines in every part,
A masterpiece of soul and heart.
No age could dull, no time could fade,
The beauty that our love has made.
Its light a gift, its glow a sign,
Of something pure, of something divine.
Together strong, we'll build this grace,
Through every trial, time, and space.
No cracks will mar, no storm will take,
The beauty that our love does make.
Forevermore, this truth will stay,
A beauty vast in every way.
The beauty of forever's hue,
Reflected bright in me and you.

Poem 59: A Love Like Fireflies

Your love, it dances in the night,
A thousand sparks of golden light.
It flickers soft, it glows with care,
A wonder rare beyond compare.
Each light a promise, soft and true,
A whispered vow from me to you.
No shadow deep, no dark too wide,
Could dim the glow where love resides.
Like fireflies in summer's breeze,
Your love brings life to tranquil seas.
It lights my path, it fills the skies,
A gentle magic in your eyes.
Together we'll embrace the glow,
A field of light that we both know.
Its brilliance vast, its beauty clear,
A love that shimmers, always near.
Forevermore, this light will stay,
A golden dance through night and day.
A love like fireflies in flight,
A tender glow, a beacon bright.

Poem 60: The Echo of Us

Our love, an echo, strong and clear,
It lingers long, it draws me near.
Each word we've shared, each truth we've known,
Resounds in hearts where seeds are sown.
The mountains hear, the valleys ring,
The echo of the love we bring.
It carries far, it reaches deep,
A sound that time will always keep.
Through every shout, through every sigh,
The echo whispers, it will not die.
It speaks of care, it hums of trust,
A voice that rises out of dust.
Together strong, our song remains,
A harmony through joys and pains.
No silence comes, no end will start,
The echo lives within our hearts.
Forevermore, the sound will play,
Through every dawn, through every day.
The echo of us, so sweet, so true,
A timeless song of me and you.

Poem 61: A Love Like the Wind

Your love, a wind that softly blows,
It moves unseen, yet everyone knows.
It lifts me high, it sets me free,
A breath of life, a mystery.
It whispers low, it calls my name,
A gentle force, a tender flame.
No wall could block, no chain could bind,
The freedom in your love I find.
Through forests deep, through skies so wide,
Your love is always by my side.
It bends the grass, it stirs the seas,
It soothes my soul, it rides the breeze.
Together we will drift and soar,
On winds of love forevermore.
No storm could take, no gale undo,
The endless wind of me and you.
Forevermore, this truth will stay,
A love like wind that finds its way.
A power vast, a force unseen,
A breeze of life where hearts convene.

Poem 62: The Thread of Forever

A thread connects us, thin but strong,
It weaves a tale where hearts belong.
Through every turn, through every mile,
It holds us close, it makes us smile.
Its fabric soft, its colors bright,
A tapestry of love's delight.
Each stitch a moment, sweet and true,
A bond that time cannot undo.
No blade could cut, no hand unweave,
The thread of love we both believe.
It stretches far, it pulls us near,
A promise held through every year.
Together we will guard this thread,
Through joys unknown, through tears we've shed.
Its strength a gift, its weave a sign,
A thread eternal, yours and mine.
Forevermore, it shall not break,
Through every step we ever take.
The thread of forever binds us tight,
A woven love, a bond of light.

Poem 63: A Love That Transcends

Our love transcends the bounds of earth,
A force eternal, of endless worth.
No limit holds, no wall contains,
A love that rises, breaks the chains.
It reaches high, it travels far,
A brilliant light, a guiding star.
Through space and time, through life's vast sea,
It bridges worlds for you and me.
No fear could halt, no pain could mar,
The love we share, our brightest star.
It bends the rules, it shifts the tide,
A boundless truth where hearts reside.
Together strong, we'll break all bounds,
Explore the depths where love resounds.
Its power vast, its truth intense,
A love that's bold, a love immense.
Forevermore, this love will be,
A journey vast, a legacy.
A love transcending time and space,
A force divine, a boundless grace.

Poem 64: A Love Like the Ocean

Your love's an ocean, deep and wide,
Its tides a force I can't divide.
It stretches far, it swells with might,
A steady flow both day and night.
Its waves caress, its currents guide,
Through every storm, through every tide.
No depths unplumbed, no shores unseen,
A boundless sea of blue and green.
Each ripple sings a soft refrain,
Of joy and peace, of loss and gain.
Its song resounds through all my days,
A melody of love's embrace.
Together, we'll traverse this sea,
A world of dreams for you and me.
No ship could sink, no gale could sway,
The ocean of love we sail each day.
Forevermore, these tides will flow,
A love so vast, we'll always know.
Its waters pure, its heart serene,
An endless ocean, vast and keen.

Poem 65: The Spark of Us

A single spark began our flame,
A flicker born from love's sweet name.
It caught the breeze, it soared so high,
A fire that lit the endless sky.
Each ember glows, each flame ascends,
A passion deep that never ends.
Its warmth a comfort, its light a guide,
A beacon bright, where dreams reside.
No storm could douse, no rain could quell,
The fire of love we know so well.
Its blaze endures, its strength remains,
A source of joy through life's domains.
Together, we will fan this fire,
A love that burns, that won't expire.
Its heat a bond, its light a vow,
A flame eternal, here and now.
Forevermore, this fire will glow,
A testament to what we know.
The spark of us, so strong, so true,
A fire of love for me and you.

Poem 66: A Love That Anchors

Your love's an anchor, strong and sure,
A steadfast force that will endure.
Through waves that crash and winds that howl,
It keeps me safe, it calms the prowl.
No storm can break, no tide can pull,
The anchor of your love so full.
It holds me firm, it keeps me near,
A haven strong, a place so clear.
Through chaos vast, through seas unknown,
Your love's a strength I've always known.
It guides my ship, it keeps me whole,
An anchor deep within my soul.
Together, we will brave the seas,
With love's strong anchor, life's sure breeze.
No force could sway, no gale could tear,
The anchor of your love and care.
Forevermore, I'll hold this trust,
An anchor strong, a bond so just.
Your love, my rock, my steady guide,
A force that keeps me by your side.

Poem 67: The Garden of Forever

Our love's a garden, lush and bright,
Where every bloom reflects the light.
Its flowers speak of care we've shown,
A world of beauty we have grown.
Each rose a moment, sweet and fair,
Each vine a bond beyond compare.
Its fragrance soft, its colors bold,
A tapestry of love untold.
Through seasons harsh, through skies unkind,
Our garden thrives, its roots entwined.
No frost could kill, no drought could fade,
The paradise that we have made.
Together, we will tend this space,
A sacred ground of love's embrace.
Each seed we plant, a promise true,
A gift of life for me and you.
Forevermore, this garden blooms,
A refuge bright through life's great rooms.
A love that grows, that will not sever,
Our garden vast, our love forever.

Poem 68: A Love That Dreams

Your love's a dream that wakes my heart,
A vision pure, a work of art.
It weaves through night, it colors day,
A dream that never fades away.
Its beauty lies in what it brings,
A world of hope, of boundless wings.
No limits bind, no borders hold,
A dream of love so bright and bold.
Through quiet nights and mornings clear,
Your love's a dream that draws me near.
It whispers soft, it glimmers bright,
A guiding star, my heart's delight.
Together, we will dream as one,
Through every moon, through every sun.
No fear could break, no doubt could mar,
The dream we share, our guiding star.
Forevermore, this dream will stay,
A light that keeps the dark at bay.
A love that dreams, that soars, that flies,
A world of hope within your eyes.

Poem 69: A Love That Binds

Our love's a bond, both firm and tight,
It weaves together day and night.
A thread of gold, it binds us near,
A tether strong, a truth sincere.
No force could break, no time unwind,
The sacred knot that we have signed.
It ties our souls, it seals our hearts,
A love that nothing breaks apart.
Through trials faced, through joys we've known,
This bond has flourished, deeply grown.
It wraps us close, it holds us fast,
A love that's built to always last.
Together, we are whole, complete,
A bond that stands through life's defeat.
No world too vast, no stars too wide,
Could break this knot where we abide.
Forevermore, this bond will stay,
A guiding force through night and day.
A love that binds, so pure, so true,
A golden thread of me and you.

Poem 70: A Love That Waits

Your love, it waits through time and space,
A constant warmth, a sweet embrace.
No need to rush, no need to run,
For love endures beneath the sun.
It knows no fear, it holds no doubt,
It waits for life to come about.
Its patience vast, its heart serene,
A steady force, a light unseen.
Through every turn, through every test,
Your love remains, it gives me rest.
Its waiting arms, its soothing care,
A quiet strength that's always there.
Together, we'll endure the years,
Through fleeting joys and fleeting tears.
Your love will wait, it will not stray,
A guiding hope, my night and day.
Forevermore, this truth will stand,
A love that waits, a steady hand.
No need for haste, no need for speed,
Your waiting love is all I need.

Poem 71: A Love That Glides

Your love, it glides on wings of grace,
It soars through every time and place.
No height too great, no sky too wide,
Could stop the flight where love resides.
It lifts me high, it sets me free,
A bird in flight, a melody.
Its feathers soft, its power strong,
A love that glides where we belong.
Through storms and winds, through clouds and rain,
Your love will guide and ease the strain.
It keeps me safe, it brings me near,
A flight of joy that's always clear.
Together, we will climb the sky,
Through endless stars where dreams will fly.
No fear could break, no night could hide,
The soaring strength of love that glides.
Forevermore, we'll take this flight,
Through every dawn, through every night.
A love that glides, so pure, so true,
A journey endless, shared with you.

Poem 72: The Glow of Your Heart

Your heart, it glows with warmth and light,
A beacon strong through darkest night.
Its brilliance shines, it draws me near,
A radiance pure, a truth sincere.
No shadow dims, no storm can fade,
The glow your loving heart has made.
It lights my path, it soothes my soul,
A tender flame that makes me whole.
Its heat a gift, its spark divine,
A steady force where hearts align.
Through every trial, through joy and tears,
Your glowing heart dispels my fears.
Together, we will share this fire,
A warmth that builds, that won't expire.
Its steady glow, its tender care,
A love that burns beyond compare.
Forevermore, your heart will shine,
A light eternal, pure, divine.
A glow that warms, that sets apart,
The endless fire within your heart.

Poem 73: A Love Like Rivers

Your love, it flows like rivers wide,
A constant stream, a faithful guide.
Through winding paths, through valleys low,
It finds its way, it always flows.
Each ripple speaks of care profound,
A soothing sound where peace is found.
No drought could halt, no dam could bind,
The flowing love so true, so kind.
It carves the stone, it shapes the land,
A gentle force, a guiding hand.
Through every bend, through every turn,
Its steady course does always yearn.
Together, we will drift and glide,
Through rivers vast, through currents wide.
No tide too fierce, no path too far,
Could halt the flow of who we are.
Forevermore, this river runs,
Beneath the moon, beneath the sun.
A love like rivers, strong and free,
A journey vast for you and me.

Poem 74: The Promise of Us

Our love is built on promises true,
A bond so strong, just me and you.
Through every storm, through every test,
It stands secure, it is our best.
Each promise made, a thread we weave,
A vow to cherish and believe.
No fleeting word, no hollow phrase,
But truths we hold through all our days.
Together, we have pledged our hearts,
A union whole, a work of art.
Each moment shared, each promise kept,
A treasure vast, where love has leapt.
No force could break, no time could sway,
The promises that guide our way.
They bind us close, they keep us near,
A love so steadfast, calm, and clear.
Forevermore, these vows will stay,
A beacon bright in night and day.
The promise of us, so strong, so pure,
A love eternal, firm, secure.

Poem 75: A Love Like Stars

Your love, it sparkles in the night,
A constellation, pure delight.
Each star a moment, bright and true,
A shining gift from me to you.
Its light unyielding, its glow profound,
A tapestry where dreams are found.
No darkness vast, no void too deep,
Could dull the stars where love does sleep.
Together, we'll explore this sky,
Through endless stars, through nights gone by.
Its beauty vast, its power immense,
A love that burns with radiance.
Each twinkle holds a whispered vow,
A love that lasts beyond the now.
No force could dim, no time could mar,
The endless glow of love's bright star.
Forevermore, the stars will say,
Our love's a light that guides the way.
A galaxy of dreams we share,
A boundless love beyond compare.

Poem 76: A Love That Reaches

Your love, it reaches far and wide,
A steady hand, a faithful guide.
No distance great, no wall too high,
Could keep it from the open sky.
It spans the earth, it touches stars,
A force that heals, that mends all scars.
No space too vast, no time too long,
Could stop the reach of love so strong.
Each hand you hold, each soul you lift,
Reflects the beauty of your gift.
Its reach a bridge through all we face,
A bond of care, a thread of grace.
Together, we will stretch and grow,
Through every path where love will go.
No limit binds, no edge can end,
A love that reaches, bends, and mends.
Forevermore, your love will span,
Through dreams unformed, through every plan.
A love that reaches, bold and true,
A gift eternal, born in you.

Poem 77: The Fire Within

Your love's a fire, deep and bright,
A blazing warmth, a vivid light.
It burns through fears, it casts away,
The shadows dark that cloud my day.
Its embers glow, they never fade,
A hearth of love that we have made.
No wind could snuff, no cold could chill,
The steady blaze of love's sweet will.
Through every trial, it keeps us warm,
A shelter strong through every storm.
Its flames ignite a passion pure,
A fire of love that will endure.
Together, we will tend this flame,
A beacon bright, a love's sweet name.
Its heat a gift, its light a vow,
A fire eternal, here and now.
Forevermore, this fire will stay,
A force that drives the dark away.
The fire within, so pure, so true,
A timeless flame that burns for you.

Poem 78: A Love That Blooms

Our love, it blooms in gentle ways,
A flower bright through all our days.
Its petals soft, its fragrance sweet,
A beauty rare, a love complete.
Each season gives its tender care,
Through sun and rain, it's always there.
Its roots run deep, its stems stand tall,
A bloom that thrives through every call.
No frost could wilt, no drought could break,
The steadfast bloom our hearts did make.
Its colors bold, its growth secure,
A love that's strong and will endure.
Together, we will tend this ground,
Where blooms of love are always found.
Through every trial, through joy and strife,
This garden grows, it springs to life.
Forevermore, this bloom will stay,
A gift of love in night and day.
A flower pure, a love that's true,
A garden vast for me and you.

Poem 79: The Canvas of Us

Our love's a canvas, bold and true,
A masterpiece of me and you.
Each brushstroke soft, each color bright,
A work of art in love's pure light.
Its hues reflect the days we share,
Each tone a testament of care.
No artist's hand could craft this grace,
A bond eternal, time won't erase.
Through every trial, every dream,
The canvas tells of love supreme.
Its beauty lies not just in part,
But in the whole, a work of heart.
Together we will paint our days,
With vivid strokes and tender praise.
A gallery of moments sweet,
Where love and life will always meet.
Forevermore, this art will show,
A masterpiece that's sure to grow.
The canvas of us, a work divine,
A portrait timeless, yours and mine.

Poem 80: The Echo of Forever

Your love, it echoes in my soul,
A sound that keeps my spirit whole.
Through mountains high, through valleys low,
It whispers truths I'll always know.
No silence deep could dim its tone,
A melody that's ours alone.
Each note a vow, each word sincere,
A harmony that draws me near.
Through every joy, through every fear,
Your love resounds, it's always clear.
No force could end its gentle song,
A music pure that lingers long.
Together, we will sing this tune,
Through every sun, through every moon.
A song of love, of joy, of peace,
A melody that will not cease.
Forevermore, its sound will play,
A serenade in night and day.
The echo of forever's hue,
A song of love for me and you.

Poem 81: A Love That Shines

Your love, it shines like morning dew,
A radiant glow, a light so true.
It fills the air, it warms the breeze,
It dances soft among the trees.
Its brilliance spreads through every part,
A golden glow within my heart.
No darkness deep, no shadow wide,
Could dim the love you hold inside.
Each smile you give, each laugh you share,
Reflects the light that's always there.
Its power vast, its beauty bright,
A guiding force through darkest night.
Together, we will share this gleam,
A radiant bond, a boundless dream.
Its glow a gift, its light so pure,
A beacon strong that will endure.
Forevermore, your love will stay,
A brilliant light in night and day.
A love that shines, so soft, so true,
A timeless glow from me to you.

Poem 82: The Journey of Us

Our love's a journey, vast and wide,
A path where hearts and dreams collide.
No road too long, no trail too steep,
A bond so strong, a vow we keep.
Each step we take, a story told,
Of love that's bright, of hearts so bold.
Through every turn, through every start,
We walk as one, with beating hearts.
No map could chart, no guide could show,
The depth of love where we will go.
Its course unknown, its way sincere,
A journey built on love and care.
Together, we will travel far,
Through distant lands, beneath the stars.
No end in sight, no goal too small,
A journey vast that captures all.
Forevermore, we'll take this way,
Through endless paths, through night and day.
The journey of us, a road divine,
A walk of love for all of time.

Poem 83: A Love That Dances

Your love, it dances in my soul,
A rhythm vast that makes me whole.
Each step a gift, each move a spark,
A waltz of joy within the dark.
No tempo rushed, no motion wild,
A gentle grace, a dance so mild.
It spins through time, it leaps through air,
A ballet sweet beyond compare.
Together, we will join the floor,
A dance of love forevermore.
No music fades, no steps will cease,
A lasting waltz of joy and peace.
Each twirl we take, each sway we find,
Reflects a love that's unconfined.
No stage too vast, no hall too grand,
A love that dances hand in hand.
Forevermore, we'll find this grace,
A dance of hearts in love's embrace.
Through every song, through life's advance,
Our love will always find its dance.

Poem 84: The River of Us

Our love's a river, deep and wide,
Its currents strong, its flow our guide.
Through every bend, through every stream,
It carries forth each shared dream.
Its waters clear, its path secure,
A steady force that will endure.
No dam could halt, no drought could dry,
The river where our hearts do lie.
Each ripple sings of journeys made,
Of memories bright that never fade.
Its voice a hymn, its course divine,
A sacred stream of yours and mine.
Together, we will ride its waves,
Through every depth, through every crave.
No storm could sway, no flood could drown,
The river love we both have found.
Forevermore, its waters flow,
A timeless truth we'll always know.
The river of us, so vast, so true,
A boundless stream of me and you.

Poem 85: A Love That Shelters

Your love's a shelter, strong and kind,
A haven safe, a peace of mind.
No storm could breach, no winds could break,
The refuge that your love does make.
Its walls are built of care profound,
A steadfast home where dreams are found.
No fear can linger, no pain can stay,
Within your arms, they fade away.
Through every trial, through every tear,
Your love protects, it keeps me near.
A fortress strong, a gentle space,
A harbor full of warm embrace.
Together, we will guard this place,
A sanctuary of endless grace.
Its strength a gift, its peace a vow,
A shelter here, forever now.
Forevermore, this home will stand,
A love secure, a life so grand.
A shelter built of hearts so true,
A sacred space for me and you.

Poem 86: The Bloom of Forever

Our love, it blooms like springtime's cheer,
A garden bright that draws me near.
Each petal soft, each fragrance sweet,
A beauty vast, a joy complete.
Its colors rich, its roots profound,
A field of love where hearts are found.
No frost could wilt, no shade could dull,
The bloom of love so bountiful.
Each season brings its tender care,
Through sunlit days and breezy air.
Our garden thrives, it will not fade,
A paradise our love has made.
Together, we will sow and reap,
A harvest full, a love so deep.
Its flowers vast, its life a glow,
A garden strong through all we know.
Forevermore, this bloom will stay,
A vibrant gift in night and day.
The bloom of forever, bold and true,
A garden bright for me and you.

Poem 87: A Love That Lingers

Your love, it lingers in my heart,
A constant force, a sacred part.
It stays through time, it does not fade,
A tender gift we both have made.
No fleeting joy, no moment's thrill,
Could match the love that lingers still.
Its touch remains, its care divine,
A lasting trace of yours and mine.
Through every breath, through every tear,
Your love remains, it draws me near.
It holds my soul, it fills my mind,
A love that's patient, strong, and kind.
Together, we will let it stay,
A love that lingers day by day.
Its presence vast, its beauty rare,
A timeless bond beyond compare.
Forevermore, this truth will shine,
A love that lingers, sweet and fine.
No force could take, no time could sever,
A love that stays with me forever.

Poem 88: The Song of Forever

Our love's a song that never ends,
A melody that time transcends.
Its notes are pure, its rhythm strong,
A hymn of life, a lasting song.
Each verse a promise, sweet and true,
A harmony of me and you.
No silence deep, no night too long,
Could stop the echo of our song.
Its tune resounds through every tear,
Through every laugh, through every year.
It speaks of joy, it hums of peace,
A symphony that will not cease.
Together, we will write each line,
A perfect chord, a love divine.
No force could break, no voice could steal,
The song of love we always feel.
Forevermore, its music plays,
A serenade through all our days.
The song of forever, soft and true,
A timeless hymn of me and you.

Poem 89: A Love That Soars

Our love takes flight on mighty wings,
A freedom sweet that soaring brings.
No cage could bind, no storm delay,
The heights of love that find their way.
It glides through clouds, it touches stars,
A journey bold, no space too far.
Each gust of wind, each lift of air,
A testament to love we share.
No mountain high, no chasm wide,
Could stop the strength of love that flies.
Its wings are built with hope and trust,
A bond eternal, strong and just.
Together, we will climb the skies,
Through endless blue, through love's sunrise.
No fear could ground, no doubt could sway,
The soaring love that finds its way.
Forevermore, our love will rise,
A flight of dreams through boundless skies.
A love that soars, so pure, so true,
A journey vast for me and you.

Poem 90: The Depths of Forever

Your love, it dives to depths unseen,
A mystery vast, a world serene.
Its waters calm, its current strong,
A force that carries hearts along.
No depth too dark, no ocean wide,
Could halt the flow where love abides.
It sinks to places rich and rare,
A treasure deep beyond compare.
Each tide it brings, a gentle song,
A lullaby where dreams belong.
Its waves embrace, its reach extends,
A bond that holds, a love that mends.
Together, we will swim these seas,
Through every depth, through every breeze.
No force could tear, no time could sever,
The depths of love that last forever.
Forevermore, this truth will stay,
A love that flows in night and day.
The depths of forever, vast and free,
A boundless sea for you and me.

Poem 91: The Strength of Together

Together we are strong and bold,
A story bright, a tale retold.
No trial too great, no test too steep,
A love that builds and vows to keep.
Each challenge faced, each burden shared,
Reflects a bond beyond compared.
Through every storm, through every fight,
We stand as one, a guiding light.
No force could break, no foe could win,
Against the strength that lies within.
Together bound, through life we sail,
A love that never will derail.
Through every path, through twists and turns,
Our love endures, it always burns.
A steady flame, a constant guide,
The strength of love we hold inside.
Forevermore, we'll stand as one,
Through every trial, until life's done.
The strength of together, bold and true,
A force eternal for me and you.

Poem 92: The Heart's Embrace

Your love's an embrace that keeps me whole,
A gentle touch that soothes my soul.
Through every fear, through every tear,
Your arms provide a world sincere.
Each time you hold, the world feels still,
A moment sweet, a tender thrill.
No fear remains, no sorrow stays,
Within your warm and loving rays.
Through every trial, through every fight,
Your heart's embrace becomes my light.
It shields my soul, it brings me peace,
A haven safe that will not cease.
Together, we will hold this space,
A sacred bond, a warm embrace.
No force could tear, no time erase,
The strength within the heart's sweet grace.
Forevermore, your arms will be,
A shelter vast for eternity.
The heart's embrace, so pure, so true,
A loving gift I find in you.

Poem 93: A Love That Heals

Your love, it heals the deepest pain,
A soothing balm through loss and gain.
Its touch is soft, its care is vast,
A force that mends, that holds steadfast.
Through every ache, through every tear,
Your love has held me, kept me near.
No wound too deep, no scar too wide,
Could hide from love that heals inside.
Its power lies in what it gives,
A gift of hope that always lives.
No broken heart, no shattered soul,
Could stay unhealed, could stay unwhole.
Together, we will face the strife,
With love that heals and gives us life.
Its strength a gift, its grace divine,
A healing love that's always mine.
Forevermore, your love will stay,
A guiding force through night and day.
A love that heals, so strong, so true,
A source of life I've found in you.

Poem 94: A Love That Glows

Your love, it glows like twilight's flame,
A gentle light, a sacred name.
It warms my soul, it fills the air,
A brilliance vast beyond compare.
Each gleam reflects the care you bring,
A glowing love, a lasting spring.
No darkness falls, no shadows stay,
Where your soft glow lights up the way.
Through every trial, through every fight,
Your love's a lantern, calm and bright.
It leads me through the roughest seas,
A steady glow, a life of ease.
Together, we will share this light,
A guiding force in darkest night.
Its glow a vow, its warmth a shield,
A love eternal, unsealed, revealed.
Forevermore, your light will shine,
A beacon strong, forever mine.
A love that glows, so pure, so true,
A brilliant light in all we do.

Poem 95: The Path of Forever

Our love's a path both clear and wide,
A journey vast where dreams reside.
No twist too sharp, no road too long,
Could shake the bond that keeps us strong.
Each step we take, a tale unfolds,
Of love that's fearless, brave, and bold.
No journey ends, no map could trace,
The path we walk in love's embrace.
Through winding turns, through trials steep,
Our hearts stay true, our promise deep.
No force could halt, no fear could sway,
The steadfast love that lights our way.
Together, we will chart this course,
Through life's great tides, through every force.
No road could break, no path could sever,
The love we walk that lasts forever.
Forevermore, this path will lead,
Through every hope, through every need.
A love eternal, pure and true,
A path unbroken for me and you.

Poem 96: A Love Like Rainbows

Your love, it shines like rainbows bright,
A spectrum vast, a vivid sight.
Its colors blend, its beauty rare,
A treasure found beyond compare.
No storm could dull, no cloud could hide,
The radiance where love resides.
It arcs through skies, it spans the seas,
A vibrant glow that sets me free.
Each hue reflects a part of you,
A heart so kind, a love so true.
Its colors sing, they softly blend,
A promise sweet that will not end.
Together, we will chase the skies,
Through endless hues where dreams arise.
No rain could wash, no doubt could fade,
The rainbow love we both have made.
Forevermore, your love will stay,
A vibrant gift in night and day.
A love like rainbows, pure and bright,
A spectrum vast, a lasting light.

Poem 97: The Touch of Forever

Your touch, it lingers on my skin,
A spark of love that lies within.
It speaks of care, it hums of peace,
A gentle strength that will not cease.
Each time we meet, each time we part,
Your touch imprints upon my heart.
No force could break, no time could steal,
The tender warmth I always feel.
Its power lies in what it gives,
A quiet truth that always lives.
No fleeting thrill, no passing rush,
Could match the grace within your touch.
Together, we will hold this vow,
Through every storm, through every now.
No time could fade, no space could sever,
The touch of love that lasts forever.
Forevermore, your hands will stay,
A soothing balm in night and day.
The touch of forever, soft and true,
A timeless bond between me and you.

Poem 98: A Love Like Morning

Your love, it wakes like morning's glow,
A quiet peace the world should know.
It greets each day with soft embrace,
A golden light, a sacred grace.
Each dawn reflects the care you bring,
A gentle start, a lasting spring.
No night could halt, no dusk could stay,
The love that rises with each day.
Through every hour, through every sun,
Your love renews, it's just begun.
No shadow deep, no dark so vast,
Could steal the light your love has cast.
Together, we will greet the dawn,
Through every sky, through every song.
A love that wakes in morning's hue,
A gift eternal, bright and true.
Forevermore, your love will rise,
A sun that lives in endless skies.
A love like morning, pure and strong,
A light that leads me all life long.

Poem 99: A Love That Surrounds

Your love, it wraps around my heart,
A sacred bond, a work of art.
It holds me close, it keeps me near,
A steady force that calms my fear.
Each touch a hug, each word a vow,
A circle endless, here and now.
No crack could form, no gap could grow,
In love's embrace that always shows.
Through every storm, through every fight,
Your love surrounds and makes things right.
No space could tear, no time could part,
The endless wrap around my heart.
Together, we will hold this grace,
A bond that time could not replace.
It wraps us tight, it keeps us whole,
A love eternal for our soul.
Forevermore, this truth will stay,
A love that wraps both night and day.
A love that surrounds, so bold, so true,
A timeless embrace from me to you.

Poem 100: The Bouquet of Love

This love we share, a blooming thing,
A gift of hearts, a song to sing.
Each flower bright, each petal rare,
A testament to all we care.
Its beauty shines through every hue,
A bond of red, of gold, of blue.
No wind could break, no storm could fade,
The bouquet bright that we have made.
Each stem a promise, bold and clear,
A love that thrives through every year.
Its roots are deep, its blooms extend,
A story vast that will not end.
Together, we will tend this field,
A love that grows, a heart revealed.
No force could take, no time could sever,
The blooms of love we'll share forever.
Forevermore, this truth will stay,
A bouquet bright through night and day.
A love eternal, vast and true,
A garden shared by me and you.